Biometrics and AI
Enhancing Security and Personal Privacy

Table of Contents

Chapter 1. Introduction

In today's digital landscape, it's never been more crucial to understand the cutting-edge technologies that shape our lives. Our Special Report delves into this rapidly evolving field, demystifying the complex yet intriguingly essential paradigm of Biometrics and AI. Despite being a highly technical topic, we've ensured to mold the insights in a down-to-earth, accessible narrative, shedding light on how these technologies enhance both security measures and personal privacy. Whether you're a novice exploring new territories or a seasoned tech-expert, this Special Report is poised to uncover something new and engaging for you. Browse through the layers of data cryptography, facial recognition algorithms, privacy law implications, and so much more, all clarified with fantastic clarity. Secure your copy now and gear up to navigate the world illuminated by the amalgamation of Biometrics and AI.

Chapter 2. Unveiling the Power of Biometrics and AI

Biometrics and Artificial Intelligence (AI) represent an enigmatic landscape of technology that feeds the growth of today's interconnected society. Both terms may sound complex, but when unfolded, it's easy to see their integration into our everyday lives, from smartphones to home security systems and beyond.

2.1. Understanding Biometrics

Biometrics refers to the measurement of biological data or physical characteristics unique to individuals. The technology measures features like fingerprints, retina patterns, voice patterns, facial structure, or even behavioral characteristics like typing rhythm. Utilizing biometrics, it's possible to accurately identify a person based on their unique traits, making it an effective security measure.

Fingerprint scanners and facial recognition systems are perhaps the most evident applications of biometric technology. These systems are now commonplace, utilized in everything from unlocking smartphones to accessing buildings. Biometric technology has even reached airports, where it is used to streamline the passport control process.

In recent years, the scope of biometric technology has expanded exponentially, moving beyond purely physical traits and examining behavioral biometrics. This explores the individual's way of interacting with technology - how one types, uses a mouse, or even walks - to provide another layer of identification.

2.2. Introduction to Artificial Intelligence

Artificial Intelligence, often referred to as AI, is another crucial piece of the puzzle. At its core, AI involves the development of computer systems that can perform tasks normally requiring human intelligence, such as understanding natural language, recognizing patterns, learning from experience, and making decisions.

AI is everywhere, driving things like Google's search algorithms, Amazon's recommendation engine, and Tesla's self-driving cars. Its capabilities range from understanding human speech with natural language processing (NLP) to recognizing images with machine vision.

In essence, AI is a tool that enables machines to mimic human intelligence and perform tasks that would typically require human cognition.

2.3. The Intersection of Biometrics and AI

When these two fields intersect, the result is an incredibly powerful tool that can significantly enhance security and personal privacy. For a simple illustration, consider unlocking your smartphone with facial recognition. The smartphone uses a biometric sensor to capture your face's image, and then AI algorithms compare this image with the one on file. If there's a match, the device unlocks.

This seamless process is the combination of biometrics and AI in action, where biometrics provides the unique personal data and AI provides the intelligence to process and make decisions based on this data.

Biometrics and AI also play a significant role in areas such as law enforcement and surveillance. Here, biometric technology is used to identify individuals in crowds through facial recognition or gait analysis. AI algorithms sift through extensive databases to match the traits captured with the corresponding individual.

2.4. Deeper into Biometrics: Data Cryptography

In a world where data breaches are increasingly common, the secure storage and handling of biometric data is critical. Enter - data cryptography, a method used to protect information by transforming it into an unreadable format.

When a biometric trait is captured, the raw data is transformed into a unique digital form using complex mathematical algorithms. This process, known as encryption, turns the easily readable data into 'cipher text,' which can only be interpreted with a 'key.' This conversion is pivotal in preventing unauthorized access to data.

Cryptography does not replace the need for safe data handling practices, but it adds a significant layer of security, enhancing overall data safety and integrity.

2.5. Unmasking Facial Recognition

Facial recognition, one of the most widely used forms of biometric technology, employs AI to identify or verify a person by comparing and analyzing patterns based on the person's facial contours.

Once the system captures an image or a video, facial recognition software focuses on key features of a person's face, such as eye position, cheekbones, or the distance between the eyes. The software then compares these captured patterns with faces in a database for a potential match.

Facial recognition has widespread applications, from unlocking smartphones to surveillance systems and tailoring personalized advertising. However, it's crucial to strike a balance between utility and privacy, making certain that the usage of such technology aligns with established privacy laws and the public's comfort level.

2.6. Exploring the Privacy Paradox

As the usage of AI and biometrics rises, so do the conversations around privacy. To reconcile the need for security with the right to privacy is a pressing concern for lawmakers, developers, and users alike.

In democratic societies, there are robust laws in place designed to protect personal data, including biometrics. But the real challenge is in balancing the requisites of security and privacy. This 'privacy paradox' – the idea that users appreciate the convenience of AI and biometric technologies but remain concerned about their personal data's safety - remains a critical issue of the digital age.

With AI and biometrics increasingly integrated into systems and services, the privacy paradox raises urgent questions that societies, industries, and legislators need to address, maintaining a fine balance between technological advancements and fundamental rights.

Biometrics and AI technology not only offer a labyrinth of security and personal benefits but also spark necessary discussions surrounding privacy. Understanding their functionalities, implications, and potential risks is imperative. The act of unveiling the powers of Biometric and AI technology is more than a need; it's an imperative journey to ensure safe navigation of our increasingly interconnected world.

Chapter 3. Exploring Different Types of Biometric Technologies

Biometric technologies harness the unique physical or behavioural characteristics of individuals for identification or access control. Over the past few years, there has been a remarkable surge in the adoption of these technologies across various sectors, including but not limited to healthcare, banking, law enforcement, and consumer electronics. While biometrics promises to enhance convenience and security, its diverse range of applications necessitates an understanding of the various types and forms it can take.

3.1. Understanding Biometric Technology

At its core, biometric technology uses statistical analysis of biological data to either identify or verify a person's identity. Despite its recent popularity, the use of biometrics isn't a novel concept; the root of biometrics dates back to ancient civilizations. Babylonians used fingerprints on clay tablets to conduct business transactions, and ancient Egyptians identified individuals based on their height. Modern biometric applications are far more complex, using sophisticated systems to analyze data on a scale not possible in ancient times.

3.2. Physiological Biometrics

Physiological biometric systems require physical evidence from the human body for identification. This evidence is often based on permanent characteristics that remain unaltered throughout an

individual's lifetime.

1. **Fingerprint scanning**: Among the most widely used biometric technologies, fingerprint scanning leverages the unique ridge-and-valley patterns on an individual's fingertips. Advanced scanners detect and analyze these minutiae points, creating a digital representation for later comparison.

2. **Facial recognition**: Employing sophisticated algorithms to identify unique patterns and features in a person's face, facial recognition is rapidly expanding in use, from mobile phone unlocking to immigration controls at airports. AI integration is enhancing its accuracy by enabling deep learning capabilities.

3. **Iris and Retina scanning**: Iris and Retina scanning involves analyzing unique patterns in a person's eyes. While Iris scanning examines the colored ring around the pupil, Retina scanning focuses on the blood vessels at the back of the eyes. These are considered among the most reliable biometric methods due to the high level of detail available for comparison.

4. **DNA profiling**: A person's DNA provides a genetic fingerprint that is utterly unique. While its use in access control situations is currently constrained by the time and resources required to conduct a test, DNA profiling is utilized extensively in forensic science.

3.3. Behavioral Biometrics

Behavioral biometrics identifies individuals based on unique patterns in their actions. Unlike physiological characteristics, behavioral traits can change over time due to aging, lifestyle alterations or even deliberate training. They offer the advantage of continuous identification and verification during user interactions.

1. **Keystroke dynamics**: This technology examines the unique manner in which a person types, including factors such as speed,

rhythm and dwell time (the time keys are kept pressed).

2. **Voice recognition**: Also known as speaker recognition, voice recognition is effective in identifying individuals by analyzing unique vocal features. While tone and pitch can be mimicked, other elements like lung capacity and vocal tract shape are difficult to duplicate.

3. **Gait analysis**: Emerging as a new area of interest, gait analysis measures one's unique walking style, including aspects like stride length and walking speed. Its passive nature – requiring no direct interaction with a user – presents new application opportunities.

4. **Signature dynamics**: Widely used in banking and financial services, signature dynamics not only compares the shape of a signature but examines the pressure applied, the writing speed, stroke order, and other aspects of the signing process.

3.4. Innovations and Future Trends

As biometric technologies continue their evolution, specialized forms are emerging. Vein pattern recognition uses near-infrared light to map the unique pattern of veins in a person's hand; heart rhythm recognition analyzes a person's unique cardiac cycle as an identifier; brainwave biometrics, still largely theoretical, could harness the unique neuro-electrical patterns generated by an individual's brain activity.

As these technologies grow in sophistication and prevalence, so too will the challenges they present. Regulatory implications, ethical debates, privacy concerns, and the potential for misuse or error will continue to shape the biometric landscape. These questions and challenges, as much as the technologies themselves, will dictate the future of biometrics in an increasingly digital, interconnected, and privacy-conscious world.

Whether they become a seamless part of our daily interactions with technology or a contentious battleground for issues of privacy and personal freedom, biometrics are set to play an influential role in the ways we verify and assert our identities in the digital landscape. By understanding these technologies — their capabilities, potentials, and risks — we can better navigate this brave new world.

Chapter 4. Deep Dive into AI Principles and Their Role in Biometrics

Biometrics is becoming intricately woven into our lives as its uses are continually broadened across various sectors in our society. This upswing can be attributed to advancements in AI technology, which underpins the principles of biometrics. This journey will take you through the understanding of the fundamental principles of artificial intelligence and how they apply in the realm of biometrics.

Chapter 5. AI and Biometrics: An Introductory Foray

Artificial intelligence (AI), in the simplest terms, refers to the simulation of human intelligence processes by machines, primarily computer systems. This technology encompasses learning (the ability to acquire and retain information), reasoning (the ability to use information to determine suitable outcomes), and self-correction, among other traits.

On the other hand, biometrics refers to the technology that uses the distinct physical characteristics or behavior to accurately identify individuals. This can include fingerprints, eye retinas and irises, voice and facial patterns, and even one's gait.

When used together, AI and biometrics can increase security measures, providing both convenience and a higher level of personal privacy.

Chapter 6. Standards and Principles: The Foundation of AI

To achieve this harmonization between AI and biometrics, specific standards and principles are established as foundations for AI based technologies.

6.1. Fairness

AI systems should be trained with fairness in mind, ensuring they do not favor one group over another. This is crucial in bio-authentication where the system should not be influenced by factors such as race, ethnicity, gender, or age. Algorithms should be reviewed regularly to ensure they maintain this standard.

6.2. Transparency

Addressing the black-box issue within AI, transparency refers to the capability to trace and see the clear routes of decision-making within an algorithm. The more transparent an AI system is, the easier it is for others to understand how outcomes were reached. In Biometrics, AI transparency can enhance trust and adoption from users by reassuring them about the systems' inner workings.

6.3. Accountability

AI systems must be accountable for their actions. That implies that if unjust actions occur, it is possible to trace them back to the component that failed. Thus, creating a fail-safe environment where errors can be identified and rectified.

6.4. Privacy and Security

In the practice of biometric identification, AI must uphold stringent privacy and security standards, safeguarding personal data and respecting individual privacy rights. Incorporating cryptographic techniques and implementing robust data protection measures are fundamental to ensure data security.

Chapter 7. AI in Action: Machine Learning and Biometrics

Machine Learning (ML), a subfield of AI, has found significant application in biometrics. ML algorithms learn patterns from large data sets and are particularly well suited for processing and learning from the wide variety of data involved in biometric systems.

7.1. Supervised Learning

In supervised learning, ML models are trained on labeled data. For biometric systems, this could be a set of images of faces, each labeled with the person's identity. The model learns defining features for each individual during training, providing identification capabilities when presented with new data.

7.2. Unsupervised Learning

While supervised learning has advantages, it requires large amounts of labeled data, which may not always be available. Unsupervised learning, on the other hand, aims to draw inferences from data sets containing input data without labeled responses. In biometrics, unsupervised learning could be used to uncover new patterns or identities by itself.

7.3. Semi-supervised Learning

Semi-supervised learning allows for learning when only a small amount of labeled data and a sizeable amount of unlabeled data are available – a more common scenario in reality. It bridges the gap between supervised and unsupervised learning and is quite relevant in biometrics, given the usual data circumstances.

Chapter 8. Bringing AI and Biometrics Unified: Neural Networks

Neural Networks, another AI subset, have brought a remarkable leap for Biometrics.

8.1. Convolutional Neural Networks

Convolutional Neural Networks (CNNs) are prevalent for image and pattern recognition tasks, including facial and fingerprint recognition. CNN incorporates layers of artificial neurons that mimic human vision processing. These networks effectively identify complex features such as contours, textures, and colors crucial in biometric identification.

8.2. Recurrent Neural Networks

Recurrent Neural Networks (RNNs) are used when we have sequences of data where the order matters. In biometric applications, gait analysis or voice recognition are two examples where RNNs shine.

This comprehensive exposition underscores how intertwined AI and Biometrics are. By understanding the principles guiding AI's application in Biometrics, we can better appreciate this innovative technology and its pivotal role in enhancing security and personal privacy. An understanding of how AI, in its diverse forms, facilitates, and drives the biometric field helps to demystify the process that seems complex at a glance. The realms of AI and Biometrics, although vast and intricate, present an exciting exploration and unmatched benefits that come with technology advent and progression.

Chapter 9. The Synergy of Biometrics and AI: Security Applications

In the digital and technological realm, the unification of biometrics and artificial intelligence (AI) spells out a new dawn in security measures. So let's descend onto this knowledgeable trail to unpack the intricate synergy of these two technologies and their growing significance in security applications.

9.1. The Fusion of Biometrics and AI: An Overview

Biometrics refers to technologies that measure and analyze individual physical or behavioral characteristics, such as fingerprints, iris patterns, or voice inflections. Over the years, biometrics has wedded with AI, thus streamlining the verification process and making it much more reliable and less time-consuming.

AI enhances the biometric capabilities by implementing machine learning algorithms that learn independently from the user's biometric inputs, hence offering higher accuracy. Such an accurate and effortless identification process ensures elevated security.

9.2. AI-Enhanced Biometric Techniques

Several biometric techniques have been improved by the infusion of AI, primarily machine learning algorithms.

9.2.1. Fingerprint Recognition

The application of AI in fingerprint recognition technology has significantly increased efficiency and accuracy. Machine learning algorithms help differentiate between partial and full fingerprints, increasing the accuracy of identification.

9.2.2. Facial Recognition

AI has become a linchpin in facial recognition. Today's advanced facial recognition systems are better equipped at identifying and interpreting essential facial features thanks to deep learning algorithms.

9.2.3. Iris Recognition

AI-powered predictive analytics, coupled with conventional iris recognition, has vastly improved this biometric technology's success rate. This biometric system is well-accepted in high-security sectors due to its non-contact nature and high accuracy.

9.3. Biometrics, AI, and Cybersecurity

In our age where cyber threats are innumerable and constantly evolving, the amalgamation of Biometrics and AI has provided an impervious layer of defense.

Machine learning algorithms automatically detect and analyze anomalies in biometric data, thus identifying potential threats. Once a threat is identified, it's managed effectively, thereby reducing data breach opportunities. Incorporating AI into biometrics yields a security measure that's proactive rather than reactive, efficiently nipping potential threats in the bud.

9.4. Enhancing User Authentication

Traditionally, usernames and passwords have been the cornerstone of user authentication. However, their vulnerability to being compromised has necessitated stronger and more foolproof methods such as biometric authentication.

AI now enables continuous and passive user authentication, a great leap forward from the traditional "login/logout" paradigm. This constant authentication ensures that only an authenticated user is accessing information or resources, thereby minimizing the chance of unapproved access.

9.5. AI Biometrics in Surveillance

The marriage of biometrics and AI in surveillance systems has resulted in vastly improved facial recognition abilities, even in diversified and vast crowds. The collection, management, and speedy interpretation of large datasets, made possible by AI, has revolutionized surveillance measures.

AI algorithms have also enabled gait recognition—the unique way a person walks—for monitoring purposes. This continuous advancement in technology is driving a shift from reactive to proactive surveillance, where AI biometrics is leveraged to predict and prevent possible threats before they actualize.

9.6. Privacy and Ethical Implications

Whilst biometrics and AI are paving the way for a secure future, they also tread on the fine line of privacy. Preserving an individual's confidentiality while ensuring the purposeful use of biometrics is a challenge faced by this technological symphony.

Tiresome are the privacy concerns surrounding biometrics and AI; however, with conscious legislation and organizations adhering to a principle-based approach, this win-win situation is feasible. Responsible use of AI and robust privacy safeguards are key to ensuring that the security benefits of biometric data do not come at the expense of individual privacy.

9.7. The Future of Biometrics and AI in Security

We're just at the dawn of this era where biometrics and AI are converging to create an almost impregnable security mechanism for digital assets, vital infrastructure, and personal data. With further refinement in AI algorithms and an increase in biometric modalities, this technology consortium's potential will continue to expand.

Traditional security measures will eventually be left in the wake of the novel and stunning efficacy of AI-empowered biometric systems. These systems, especially when they are lucidly regulated and utilized, will evolve into the penultimate line of defense in digital security.

In essence, biometrics and AI's combined capabilities have shown what a formidable team they make for security applications. There is immense scope for these technologies to further evolve, mature, and redefine the future of security across numerous spectrum of life. Although the path summoning these technologies together might have its obstacles, their seamless integration yields a world of potential that is simply too beneficial to surrender.

I hope this comprehensive exploration of the correlation between biometrics and AI in security applications illuminates their importance and potential in the ever-evolving technological landscape. As we move forward, these developments promise not only a secure digital environment but also, perhaps more importantly, blend this security with preserving the sanctity of personal privacy.

Chapter 10. Unlocking the Potential of Facial Recognition Technology

Facial recognition technology, the automated process that identifies or verifies an individual's identity using their face, represents one of the most rapidly evolving branches within the biometrics and artificial intelligence space. It captures, analyzes, and compares patterns based on the individual's facial details.

10.1. Understanding the Mechanics

At the heart of facial recognition technology is the need to identify or verify an individual's face. This process involves the detection and mapping of physical features from an image or video. Software algorithms then compare this information with stored data in a database.

In technical terms, the process can be broken down into several steps:

1. Detecting a face in the stream of input, which might come from photographs or videos.

2. Processing the detected face to capture unique features such as the shape and size of the eyes, nose, cheekbones, and jawline, which form the faceprint.

3. Encoding the faceprint into a compact yet comprehensive template.

4. Matching this template with existing ones in the database.

Each of these steps utilizes highly sophisticated techniques driven by artificial intelligence and machine learning algorithms. The template creation, in particular, uses an AI technique called deep learning, which, over the past few years, has significantly advanced the accuracy of facial recognition technology.

10.2. Bridging Biometrics and AI

Today, we are seeing a rise in AI-driven biometrics, such as facial recognition. This rise integrates the AI phenomenon with the unique traits of each individual, making identification processes more accurate and reliable. Artificial intelligence plays a vital role in enhancing the efficiency and effectiveness of biometric technologies as it provides the necessary 'intelligence' to comprehend complex patterns and variations in biometric data.

In the context of facial recognition, the convergence of AI and biometrics provides an integral framework for identification processes. Machine learning algorithms, a subset of AI, enable the system to learn from sample face images, making the technique more accurate over time.

10.3. Real-world Applications

Facaced with a rapidly evolving digital landscape, facial recognition technology is finding usage beyond the typical domains of security and law enforcement. Industries across the spectrum are exploring novel applications of this technology, changing how companies and consumers interact.

Several real-world applications have emerged:

1. **Customized advertising:** Using facial recognition, advertisers can gauge the age, gender, and even emotions of people viewing their ads, allowing them to tailor the advertisement to the viewer's profile.

2. **Healthcare:** Facial recognition has enormous potential for

patient identification, reducing the chances of misidentification errors while maintaining privacy.

3. **Retail:** Retail stores can use facial recognition to identify repeat customers or shoplifters. By analyzing facial expressions, retailers can also harness insights into shopper sentiments.

4. **Education:** Institutions are embracing facial recognition to monitor classroom attendance systems, ensuring student attention and participation while respecting privacy protocols.

10.4. Privacy and Security Implications

While the promise of facial recognition technology is undeniable, its widespread use also raises pertinent questions about privacy and security. Regulatory frameworks worldwide are grappling with defining and enforcing the right norms for AI and biometric technologies.

Facial recognition technology deals with highly sensitive data, which makes it a tempting target for malicious cyber activities. Security breaches can lead to misuse of stored facial data, causing severe personal and financial harm.

On the privacy front, the omnipresence of facial recognition technology can lead to unwarranted surveillance and monitoring, infringing upon civil liberties. Consequently, it is crucial to strike a balance between leveraging the benefits of these technologies and safeguarding human rights.

10.5. The Road Ahead

The future of facial recognition technology continues to unfold with newer advancements and a greater understanding of its implications. As we continue exploring its potential, the concerns surrounding privacy and security cannot be ignored. Therefore, safeguards like transparent data usage policies, rigorous cybersecurity measures, robust legal frameworks, and ongoing public discourse will be of paramount importance.

As the intersection of AI and biometrics continues to redefine facial recognition technology, we can only anticipate these changes with both optimism for the colossal potential and due diligence towards challenges therein. Thus, unlocking the potential of facial recognition technology requires an intricate dance of judicious technological usage, and constant vigilance regarding its societal implications.

Chapter 11. Use of Biometric AI in Fraud Detection and Prevention

The advent of Biometric AI in matters relating to fraud detection and prevention is a key development in digital technology. It's a strategic addition to the security layers of any organization, monitoring and evaluating user actions to detect anomalies and prevent potential threats. Biometric AI necessitates a unique, unobtrusive method of assessing users, contrasting with traditional modes of authentication that demand username and passwords, which are susceptible to being guessed, stolen, or exploited.

11.1. Biometric AI: The Basics

Biometric AI draws on artificial intelligence to enhance the utilization of biometric systems. These systems assess individual identifying traits — such as facial structure, retina, fingerprints, or behavioral characteristics like keystroke dynamics and gait analysis. AI algorithms underlying these systems categorize and store data, subsequently comparing it with real-time user data to verify identity.

11.2. Evolution of Biometric AI

The evolution of Biometric AI was primarily driven by the need for enhanced security protocols, especially in the digital realms where the conventional authentication methods marked an upsurge in fraudulent activities. The integration of artificial intelligence and biometrics brought along an incredibly secure, robust, non-transferable, and distinctive method of authentication, an advancement that has revolutionized security and fraud prevention systems.

Biometric technology began with traditional fingerprint scanning, used primarily for criminal investigations. The shift to digital platforms saw an expansion of this technology to include other physiological and behavioral characteristics such as iris patterns, voice recognition, and keystroke dynamics. Artificial intelligence entered the fray to refine how these biometrics were processed, stored, and compared, adding an unprecedented level of precision.

11.3. Types of Biometric AI

There are several types of Biometric AI technologies currently in use:

1. **Fingerprints**: This involves scanning the unique ridges and valleys on a finger's surface.

2. **Facial recognition**: This applies deep learning algorithms to analyze facial features.

3. **Iris recognition**: A less common but highly secure method, examining the unique patterns in a person's iris.

4. **Voice recognition**: This analyses the voice patterns, tone, pitch and other vocal traits for identification.

5. **Behavioral biometrics**: This extends to the patterns of behavior, including keystroke dynamics, gait analysis, etc.

11.4. Biometric AI in Fraud Detection

The adoption of biometric AI in fraud detection operates on the premise of real-time threat analysis and evaluation. The AI-based biometric systems identify anomalies that may represent potential security threats, e.g., unauthorized access attempts, abnormal user behavior, or failed multiple logins.

These systems don't just stop at identity authentication; they also actively learn and adapt to new patterns and threats. This adaptive learning comes courtesy of machine learning algorithms, enabling the system to distinguish between innocent anomalies and probable fraudulent activities.

For example, suppose a user who usually logs in during the day suddenly attempts to access the system late at night. In that case, the behavioral biometric AI will flag this as anomalous behavior, triggering an alert.

11.5. Biometric AI For Fraud Prevention

Fraud prevention goes beyond detecting and responding to threats; it involves pre-emptive strategies to mitigate the risks of fraudulent activity. Biometric AI plays an instrumental role here.

The predictive capabilities of artificial intelligence allow it to not only detect potential threats but also forecast future ones based on the available data patterns. Because of its machine learning nature, it continually learns from previous incidents, improving its proficiency in identifying and preventing future threats.

When it comes to physical fraud prevention, biometric AI is irreplaceable. For instance, fingerprint or facial recognition is uniquely tied to an individual, thus eliminating the risk of passcodes being shared or stolen.

11.6. Challenges for Biometric AI

While the advantages are numerous, biometric AI also faces challenges. These include:

1. **Data privacy concerns**: As this technology involves collecting sensitive personal data, misuse can result in severe violations.

2. **System vulnerabilities**: While robust, there's always a risk of security loopholes which may be exploited by potential hackers.

3. **False positives**: Biometric systems may sometimes flag innocent activities as threats, leading to unnecessary disruption.

4. **Future-proofing**: Technology is constantly evolving, increasing the demand for biometric AI systems to keep pace.

11.7. Future of Biometric AI in Fraud Detection & Prevention

The future points toward even greater integration of Biometric AI into fraud detection and prevention systems. With continued advancements, we can expect more sophisticated iterations of the technology, offering increased security and minimization of fraud.

Despite the challenges, the prospects for Biometric AI in fraud detection and prevention appear promising. As the technology evolves and advances, both in terms of hardware for biometrics data collection and the AI algorithms that process this data, the result will be more sophisticated, accurate, and secure systems.

Securing digital assets is no longer a luxury, but a fundamental necessity. Biometric AI has demonstrated its potential in enhancing cyber-security, and in doing so, has redefined traditional approaches to fraud detection and prevention. Despite the technicality of the subject, understanding and leveraging its capabilities can significantly mitigate organizations' security risks. To stay ahead, every business must look beyond traditional security measures and incorporate the advanced techniques that Biometric AI has to offer.

Chapter 12. Understanding the Importance of Personal Privacy in the Digital Age

The digital age has brought about unprecedented changes, transforming the way we live, learn, and interact. As our worlds increasingly converge with technology, it's vital to understand the shifts in personal privacy paradigms for their broader implications on security, autonomy, social structures, and democracy.

12.1. Defining Personal Privacy

At its core, personal privacy is the presumption that individuals should have the right to withhold themselves or information about themselves from public view. In the digital context, privacy takes on different nuances. It extends to data protection and pertains to the collection, use, storage, and dissemination of personal data.

Online interactions leave a trail of digital footprints. These footprints may include identifiable information (name, address, email), financial data (credit card, bank details), digital behavior (search queries, clicks, likes), and even biometric data (facial recognition, fingerprint).

12.2. Privacy Matters: Why Is Digital Privacy Essential?

Digital privacy is crucial as it lays the foundation for several essential attributes of democratic society. Here are the key reasons to consider:

Autonomy: With privacy, individuals have the freedom to engage in activities without being monitored. It allows for personal growth and self-exploration in the digital realm.

Freedom of Expression: Privacy supports freedom of speech and thought. Without it, people may be hesitant to voice their opinions or engage in discussions for fear of surveillance or judgments.

Dignity and Reputation: Individuals should control how personal information is depicted online. Any breach may lead to misrepresentation or misuse, potentially damaging an individual's dignity and reputation.

Data Security: As personal data becomes valuable in industries like marketing and research, it also becomes a target for cybercriminals. Maintaining privacy helps to guard against identity theft, fraud, cyberstalking, and other related crimes.

12.3. Digital Privacy and Surveillance: A Delicate Balance

While privacy is essential, it can sometimes collide with the need for surveillance to counteract risk factors like terrorism, crime, or even public health threats. Significant concerns arise around the balance of these two competing interests - privacy of the individual and public safety provided by surveillance.

For example, our society is divided about the use of CCTVs, facial recognition technology, or AI-powered surveillance systems. While these systems have demonstrated efficacy in dealing with crime and security threats, there's an ongoing conversation about how these technologies infringe on privacy.

12.4. Regulatory Frameworks Protecting Digital Privacy

To address these concerns, several legal doctrines at national and international levels work together to protect individuals' digital privacy rights.

The **General Data Protection Regulation (GDPR)** in EU law is a prime example. GDPR applies to all companies that process the data of subjects residing in the EU, offering residents control over their personal data. Under this regulation, organizations are required to protect personal data from misuse and respect individuals' rights for privacy.

In the United States, several federal laws offer privacy protection in various sectors, such as the Health Insurance Portability and Accountability Act (HIPAA) for health information, or the Children's Online Privacy Protection Act (COPPA) for children's data.

12.5. The Role of Biometrics and AI in Digital Privacy

As biometrics and AI technologies become ever more pervasive, they carry both prospects and perils for digital privacy. On the positive side, biometrics can offer robust security measures, preventing unauthorized access to personal information. AI can also enhance privacy protection through advanced fraud detection or encryption techniques.

Yet, these technologies can also threaten privacy. Collecting biometric data might be intrusive, and there's a risk of misuse if that data falls into the wrong hands. AI can be employed in large-scale surveillance systems which may infringe on individual privacy.

Therefore, it's critical to ensure that these technologies are designed and deployed with privacy protections in mind and under legal or ethical guidelines.

12.6. Evolving Digital Privacy: A Path Forward

Privacy in the digital world isn't a fixed concept but continues to evolve with technological and societal shifts. As we look ahead, there are a few key trends:

Privacy-by-design: Technology companies are recognizing the need to build privacy into their technology structures from the start. This idea, often called "Privacy by Design," incorporates privacy measures in the design phase of a product or service.

Decentralised identity systems: As an alternative to centrally held data, decentralized identity systems allow individuals to verify their own identity, hold their data, and choose when and where to share that data.

Coding laws into technology: In the future, technology could encode privacy laws, with machines programmed to respect privacy norms.

In conclusion, privacy continues to be a provocative, complex issue in the digital age. Respectful discourse, regulatory oversight, and privacy-minded tech design are a must to navigate the dual requirements of protection and liberty. As biometrics and AI increasingly become part of our everyday lives, the necessity to balance these intricate aspects will undoubtedly continue to be a pivotal challenge and opportunity. Therefore, the old adage, "Knowledge is power," holds true here - individuals informed about their digital privacy rights ultimately shape more secure digital societies.

Chapter 13. Legal Implications and Privacy Laws Around Biometric AI

In our increasingly interconnected, digital society, biometric artificial intelligence (AI) has emerged as both a beneficial tool and a source of legal complexity. This technology, which analyses physical or behavioral characteristics unique to an individual to confirm identity or grant access, brings with it wide-ranging implications spanning across ethics, privacy, legality, and more.

13.1. Introduction to Biometric AI and Privacy Laws

Understanding the legal implications of biometric technology's usage and the surrounding privacy laws requires some foundational knowledge. The incorporation of AI into biometrics has enabled more sophisticated administration of personal identification, enhancing security but simultaneously presenting several challenges. Algorithms can now accurately analyze and predict personal and behavioral traits, such as facial patterns, iris structures, and voice syntax. However, the extraction, storage, usage, and disposal of such sensitive data have raised critical privacy and legal affairs worldwide, prompting stringent laws and regulations.

13.2. History and Evolution of Privacy Laws

The history of privacy laws, notably in the context of digital data, dates back to the late 20th century. The enactment of the Data Protection Act in 1984 by the United Kingdom, later replaced in 2018, ushered privacy and data protection into the legal spectrum. Similar trends were observed around the world, with the United States, Australia, and other nations instituting laws to keep up with digital advancements. The advent of biometric AI has necessitated corresponding updates to these laws, reacting to the heightened sensitivity and potential misuse of biometric data.

13.3. Key Global Privacy Regulations and Biometric Data

Several key global regulations have nuanced implications for biometric AI. From General Data Protection Regulation (GDPR) in the European Union, which introduced stringent measures to regulate the data handling, to the California Consumer Privacy Act (CCPA) that grants California's residents an array of data-related rights. Other countries, such as India's Personal Data Protection Bill (PDPB), are also framing rules for data localization, data minimization, and explicit consent.

These regulations all share a common thread – the affirmative need for individual consent for the collection, storage, and usage of biometric data.

13.4. Informed Consent in Biometric Data Collection

'Informed consent' is a pillar of the legal framework surrounding biometrics. It's an ethical and legal obligation to communicate the intent, benefits, risks, and alternatives associated with the collection and use of biometric data. The individual must also have the autonomy to accept, reject, or later revoke consent. Unauthorized collection, third-party sharing without permission, or non-disclosure of data breaches could lead to harsh penalties, reflecting the gravity ascribed to consent.

13.5. Case Laws and Legal Precedents

Analyzing case laws and legal precedents offers insights into privacy laws' implementation under the biometric AI landscape. Landmark cases such as 'Facebook's Biometric Privacy Lawsuit' (2020), where Facebook agreed to pay a $650 million settlement for allegedly breaching Illinois Biometric Information Privacy Act (BIPA), and 'Google's Facial Recognition Class Action Lawsuit' (2020) have highlighted the complexities even tech giants face around data ethics and privacy implications, shaping the current legal canvas.

13.6. Profiling and Decision Making

One aspect of biometric AI, attracting legal and ethical scrutiny, is the concept of 'profiling' - automated processing of personal data to analyze or predict aspects about an individual. Profiling could lead to discriminatory, biased outcomes or breach privacy rights, consequently violating GDPR and similar legislation. It's essential that transparency, human intervention, accuracy, and the right to contest decisions are ensured in such processes.

13.7. Law Enforcement Access to Biometric Data

The interface of law enforcement with biometric data calls into review another set of legal concerns. While crime investigation and national security can benefit from biometric data, it raises questions around unwarranted surveillance, privacy infringements, and misuse. Here, balancing the potential societal benefits against personal liberties presents a challenge to the legal framework.

13.8. Future Legal Implications

While existing regulations provide a basis for biometric AI's legal groundwork, future legal implications will depend on the evolving nature of technology, societal norms, and regulatory environments. The possibility of exploiting biometric data through deepfakes, blending of virtual reality with biometrics, increase in telemedicine, and advent of quantum computing would usher in unexplored legal territories demanding foresight and proactive legislation.

Navigating the intricacies of biometric AI and privacy laws highlights the vital balance needed between technological advancement and personal privacy. Governments worldwide need to establish transparent, robust, and comprehensive laws, ensuring ethical practices while enabling this powerful technology's advantages.

Chapter 14. Emerging Trends in Biometric and AI Technologies

As we navigate through the oscillating currents of the rapidly advancing digital landscape, it hinges substantially on our understanding of the nuances of new-age technologies. Among these, Biometrics and AI have redefined how we view security and personal privacy. As much complex as they might appear on the surface, an immersive peeling back of the layers reveals a fascinating world of data, algorithms, and legal implications. Let's sift through these layers, exploring the emerging trends in these fields.

14.1. The Evolution of Biometrics and AI

Over the last few decades, Biometrics and AI have progressively evolved. Once a concept read about only in futuristic sci-fi novels, they've now become integral to many parts of our daily lives. Biometrics, like fingerprints or facial recognition, paired with potent AI algorithms, are now employed for unlocking smartphones, passing through airport security, verifying identities during online transactions, and much more.

However, we're only just scratching the surface of what these technologies can accomplish. As their capabilities expand, so will their roles in our lives. From securely facilitating seamless digital transactions to even predicting potential health challenges, the potential applications seem nearly limitless.

14.2. Increasing Accuracy and Recognizing Emotions

The precision of biometric systems is increasingly being augmented, largely due to advancements in AI. The most promising area of growth lies in the AI sub-field of machine learning, where computers learn to improve tasks based on experience, refining their ability to recognize patterns and improving accuracy over time.

Efforts in emotion recognition and prediction are also taking shape in the modern technology landscape, with biometrics and AI at the helm. An AI system can analyze facial expressions and voice patterns to infer an individual's mood or emotional state, having broad implications in fields such as advertising, customer service, or mental health.

14.3. Biometric Data Security and Data Cryptography

Significant challenges lie in ensuring the security of the biometric data that we increasingly rely on. The evolving landscape of cyber security threats mandates rigorous data encryption measures.

Data cryptography plays a significant role in biometric technology, ensuring the secure transmission and storage of sensitive data. This involves the conversion of readable data (plain text) into a code (cipher text) to prevent unauthorized access. When deciphered using a specific key, the information is restored to its readable form, making it a powerful tool in preventing identity theft and data breaches.

14.4. Embracing AI for Enhanced Privacy Laws

The advent and progression of AI and biometrics have opened a cumulative can of worms regarding personal privacy. While these technologies have the potential to greatly strengthen personal and national security, a delicate balance must be struck to ensure personal privacy isn't compromised.

Government and private institutions are therefore looking to AI itself to proactively guard against privacy violations. For instance, AI systems can be trained to redact sensitive information from public documents or videos, or alert users when their personal data is being shared without their knowledge or consent.

14.5. Integrating Deepfake Detection

The unprecedented growth in AI technologies has seen the rise of 'deepfakes' - false yet realistic images or videos generated by sophisticated AI systems. The era of deepfakes presents a serious threat to personal privacy and security.

To combat this, technologies are being developed to improve detection of deepfakes, with AI playing a key role in these countermeasures. Advanced machine learning techniques are being used to identify inconsistencies and abnormalities in visuals and audio that would be unnoticeable to the human eye and ear.

Emerging trends in biometric and AI technologies are shaping our present while promising an exciting future. With these advancements, we are progressively creating a world where technology is not merely a tool, but an ally. Understanding and embracing these changes is pivotal for our journey ahead in this digital age.

Chapter 15. Future Prospects and Challenges of Biometric AI

The future landscape of Biometric AI is both promising and daunting, a frontier laden with incredible potential opportunities and complexities. As we delve deeper into a digital world increasingly defined by artificial intelligence, it is paramount to anticipate the road ahead with a clear and informed perception.

15.1. Technological Advances and Innovations

Technological advancements typically drive the evolution of Biometric AI. Cutting-edge innovations have enhanced efficiencies, improved the accuracy of biometric systems, and opened up a flurry of new applications.

Biometric AI is already extending beyond conventional modalities, such as fingerprinting, face recognition, and iris scanning. Newer recognition techniques, such as heart rhythm recognition, gait analysis, and brainwave identification, are gradually being explored, promising to provide even more secure, non-intrusive, and personalized identification processes.

Simultaneously, convergences of AI, Internet of Things (IoT), and 5G technology are set to accelerate the deployment of more large-scale, versatile, and real-time biometric systems. Combining high-speed, low-latency 5G networks with IoT devices will allow the transmission and analysis of biometric data in real-time, boosting the efficiency of the systems and potentially pervading every facet of daily life.

15.2. The Dawn of Behavioral Biometrics

Behavioral biometrics is a rapidly emerging field, focusing on identifiable patterns in human activity. This discipline looks at distinctive characteristics like keystroke dynamics, voice cadence, signature formation, mouse movements, and even the unique way users interact with devices.

Here, machine learning algorithms can learn, make sense of, and recognize individual behavior patterns, providing another layer of security. The value proposition extends beyond authentication by also offering continual verification, keeping checks even after the initial login. This could potentially revolutionize cybersecurity, providing robust, continuous security without disrupting user experiences.

15.3. Personalized Experiences – A New Normal

Biometric AI is steering the world towards hyper-personalization, potentially shifting how services and products are experienced and delivered. Companies can leverage this technology to tailor-fit experiences according to user profiles, improving customer satisfaction and increasing brand loyalty.

Conversely, the rise of digital personal assistants, given their ability to learn and recognize behavioural, voice, and other biometric patterns, will lead to more personal and intuitive experiences.

15.4. Biometric AI and Public Services

Recognizing the power of biometric technology, governments worldwide are integrating it into public services. For instance, the adoption of biometric National ID systems is rising, helping to streamline governance, reduce fraud, and enhance service provision.

The realm of public security is witnessing innovations with biometric AI, from surveillance systems employing facial recognition to predictive policing strategies using data analysis. These, while improving public safety, pose significant questions on personal privacy and system misuses.

15.5. Privacy Concerns and Regulatory Challenges

While the advancements in Biometric AI are laden with immense potential, they bring alongside serious concerns. Notably, personal privacy stands at the fault lines of this digital revolution. With more personal data shared, stored, and used, the risk of misuse increases, a concern that is heightened given the sensitive nature of biometric information.

This ushers in an urgent need for regulatory measures that balance the technical progress with ethical and privacy considerations. The challenge lies in formulating regulations that do not suffocate innovation, yet provide a robust data protection policy and practice.

In this vein, the General Data Protection Regulation (GDPR) from the European Union stands as a landmark. However, differing privacy laws around the globe pose considerable challenges to biometric AI's universal application, needing reconciliation of conflicting legal landscapes.

15.6. The Risk of Deepfakes

A notable challenge to biometric AI is the rise of "deepfakes", synthetic media content created using AI techniques. Deepfakes pose significant security risks as they can trick biometric systems and lead to misinformation or identity theft, posing severe social and personal implications.

This threat calls for an increase in developing techniques to distinguish between real and artificial entities. Here again, AI technology finds itself at the core of finding solutions, creating an unprecedented challenge tinged with irony.

To summarize, the future of Biometric AI is an exciting realm filled with immense potential. Still, it calls for careful navigation and vigilant regulation. Unbridled growth sans oversight can lead to risky implications, whereas over control could stifle innovation. The optimal way forward is to strike a measured balance, ensuring that while we boldly navigate this brave new world, we do not lose sight of the principles that anchor us to our shared humanity.

www.ingramcontent.com/pod-product-compliance
Lightning Source LLC
Chambersburg PA
CBHW061054050326
40690CB00012B/2616